Sepulch.

CW00552526

Sepulchres

Ugo Foscolo

Translated by

J.G. Nichols

ALMA CLASSICS

ALMA CLASSICS LTD
Hogarth House
32-34 Paradise Road
Richmond
Surrey TW9 1SE
United Kingdom
www.almaclassics.com

The poem 'Sepulchres' first published in *Translation and Literature* with the title 'Of Tombs' in 1995, and subsequently included in *Last Letters of Jacopo Ortis*, published by Hesperus Press Limited in 2002.
First published by Alma Classics Limited (previously Oneworld Classics Limited) in 2009
This new edition first published by Alma Classics Limited in 2015

English translation of 'Sepulchres' © J.G. Nichols, 1995, 2002, 2009
All other English translations © J.G. Nichols, 2009
Notes and extra material © J.G. Nichols, 2009

This book is published with the support of the Italian Ministry of Foreign Affairs.

Printed by CreateSpace

ISBN: 978-1-84749-466-5

Contents

Sepulchres

Sonnets

Solcata ho fronte, occhi incavati intenti,   1
crin fulvo, emunte guance, ardito aspetto,
labbro tumido acceso, e tersi denti,
capo chino, bel collo, e largo petto;

giuste membra, vestir semplice eletto;
ratti i passi, i pensier, gli atti, gli accenti;
sobrio, umano, leal, prodigo, schietto;
avverso al mondo, avversi a me gli eventi:

talor di lingua, e spesso di man prode;
mesto i più giorni e solo, ognor pensoso,   10
pronto, iracondo, inquïeto, tenace:

di vizi ricco e di virtù, do lode
alla ragion, ma corro ove al cor piace:
morte sol mi darà fama e riposo.

I*

A furrowed brow, eyes staring and sunk deep;   1
Hair tawny, cheekbones showing through, bold-faced;
Lips that are full and red, with gleaming teeth;
Head bent, a fine-set neck and a broad chest;

Good limbs, clothes that are choice and plain and neat;
Rapid in walking, thoughts, deeds, what I say;
Sober, humane, loyal, prodigal and straight;
Cold to the world, which turns away from me;

Sometimes in speech, and often brave in deed;
Sad most days and alone, thoughtful at best,   10
Prompt, and quick to be angry, restless, strong;

Rich in virtues and vice, I praise and laud
Reason, but, where my heart goes, go along:
And only death will give me fame and rest.

Non son chi fui – perì di noi gran parte: 1
questo che avanza è sol languore e pianto.
E secco è il mirto, e son le foglie sparte
del lauro, speme al giovenil mio canto.

Perché dal dì ch'empia licenza e Marte
vestivan me del lor sanguineo manto,
cieca è la mente e guasto il core, ed arte
la fame d'oro, arte è in me fatta, e vanto.

Ché se pur sorge di morir consiglio,
a mia fiera ragion chiudon le porte   10
furor di gloria, e carità di figlio.

Tal di me schiavo, e d'altri, e della sorte,
conosco il meglio ed al peggior mi appiglio,
e so invocare e non darmi la morte.

II*

I am not what I was – so much is lost: 1
Nothing remains but to lament and weep.
Myrtle* is withered, and those leaves dispersed
That crowned the laurel,* once my youthful hope.

Since Mars and irresponsible revolt
Mantled me, as they always do, in blood,
I have been blind, heartbroken, and my art
A thirst for gold, of which I'm all too proud.

And even when I think it best to die,
The door to this proud purpose is slammed shut   10
By rage for fame, and filial piety.

Slave to myself, to others and to fate,
I take the worse, though see the better way,
And call on death, and yet fight shy of it.

Forse perché della fatal quïete   1
tu sei l'immago a me sì cara vieni
o Sera! E quando ti corteggian liete
le nubi estive e i zeffiri sereni,

e quando dal nevoso aere inquïete
tenebre e lunghe all'universo meni,
sempre scendi invocata, e le secrete
vie del mio cor soavemente tieni.

Vagar mi fai co' miei pensier su l'orme
che vanno al nulla eterno; e intanto fugge   10
questo reo tempo, e van con lui le torme

delle cure onde meco egli si strugge;
e mentre io guardo la tua pace, dorme
quello spirto guerrier ch'entro mi rugge.

III*

Is it because you seem the very sister   1
Of our fatal quiescence you are dear,
O Evening? Whether courted by a cluster
Of summer clouds and gentle zephyrs, or

Whether from snow-filled skies you slowly loose
Long-lasting shadows on the troubled world,
You always come invoked, and softly trace
Those secret ways in which my heart's enthralled.

You send my contemplation wandering
Towards eternal nothingness. Time flies,   10
This bad time flies, and with it bears along

This band of cares, killing me as it dies.
And while I look upon your peace, you bring
Peace to the spirit that within me roars.

E tu ne' carmi avrai perenne vita   1
sponda che Arno saluta in suo cammino
partendo la città che del latino
nome accogliea finor l'ombra fuggita.

Già dal tuo ponte all'onda impäurita
il papale furore e il ghibellino
mescean gran sangue, ove oggi al pellegrino
del fero vate la magion si addita.

Per me cara, felice, inclita riva
ove sovente i pie' leggiadri mosse   10
colei che vera al portamento Diva

in me volgeva sue luci beate,
mentr'io sentia dai crin d'oro commosse
spirar ambrosia l'aure innamorate.

IV*

And you in poetry will live for ever,   1
Bank that the Arno kisses as it flows
And cuts in two that city* which displays
Some shadow still of ancient Latin lustre.

Once from your bridge to waters in their fright
The papal fury and the Ghibelline*
Shed floods of blood, where now to travelled men
The home of the fierce bard* is pointed out.

Happy bank, dear to me and known to Fame,
Where oftentimes her graceful footsteps went   10
Who by her bearing showed she was divine,

Whose eyes blessed me when I felt she was near
And I was conscious of the ambrosial scent
From winds enamoured of her lifted hair.

Un dì, s'io non andrò sempre fuggendo 1
di gente in gente, me vedrai seduto
su la tua pietra, o fratel mio, gemendo
il fior de' tuoi gentili anni caduto.

La madre or sol, suo dì tardo traendo,
parla di me col tuo cenere muto,
ma io deluse a voi le palme tendo
e sol da lunge i miei tetti saluto.

Sento gli avversi numi, e le secrete
cure che al viver tuo furon tempesta, 10
e prego anch'io nel tuo porto quïete.

Questo di tanta speme oggi mi resta!
Straniere genti, almen le ossa rendete
allora al petto della madre mesta.

V*

One day, if I do not go fleeing on   1
From land to land, you will find me in tears
Over your tomb, my brother,* as I mourn
The withered flower of your most noble years.

Our mother, seeing life out all alone,
Talks to your silent ashes about me,
While I stretch hands and heart to you in vain,
Greeting my house and home but distantly.

I feel the adverse fates, and the repressed
Troubles that thundered through your living veins,   10
And pray that in your haven I may rest.

Today of all my hopes but this remains!
O foreign peoples, send my bones at least
Back to the breast of her who always mourns.

Né più mai toccherò le sacre sponde   1
ove il mio corpo fanciulletto giacque,
Zacinto mia, che te specchi nell'onde
del greco mar da cui vergine nacque

Venere, e fea quelle isole feconde
col suo primo sorriso, onde non tacque
le tue limpide nubi e le tue fronde
l'inclito verso di colui che l'acque

cantò fatali, ed il diverso esiglio
per cui bello di fama e di sventura   10
baciò la sua petrosa Itaca Ulisse.

Tu non altro che il canto avrai del figlio,
o materna mia terra: a noi prescrisse
il fato illacrimata sepoltura.

VI*

No, I'll not land upon your sacred shore,   1
Zante, ever again! My earliest years
Were spent on you, mirrored in water where
Out of the Grecian waves the goddess rose,

Venus our nurse, and fructified the isles
With her first smile! And he* did not forget
The clear clouds and thick foliage in your skies
In his famed verse,* he who knew how to set

In song the fatal seas, the various
Toils, till he kissed his rocky Ithaca,   10
Of Ulysses, one not unknown to fame.

You will have nothing left you but the verse
Your child sings, O my mother's land! My doom
Is exile and an unwept sepulchre.

Fugitive Pieces
and Odes

Contro Lamberti

"Che fa Lamberti   1
uomo dottissimo?"
"Stampa un Omero
laboriosissimo."
"Commenta?" "No."
"Traduce?" "Oibò.
Le prime prove ripassando va,
ed ogni mese un foglio dà,
talché in dieci anni lo finirà –
se pur Bodoni pria non morrà."   10
"Lavoro eterno!"
"Paga il governo."

*Against Lamberti**

"What is Lamberti doing,   1
That learned man?"
"Printing a Homer
He works hard upon."
"Does he comment?" "Oh no!"
"Does he translate?" "Oh! Oh!
He is revising his first proof,
And issues every month one leaf;
We'll see it end with the decade;
Unless Bodoni is already dead."   10
"That is a work undying!"
"The Government is paying."

A Leopoldo Cicognara

Stampi chi vuole sue prosacce in rima: 1
tu con Lucia gentil leggi sì piano
questa, che in altre orecchie non s'imprima.

Non so ch'uomo giammai ponesse mano
a una commedia che ribrezzo e riso
insiem ti desti contro un mostro umano.

E' pare che Natura abbia diviso
dalla lepida beffa il raccapriccio:
aborri Giuda, e ridi di Narciso.

Pure a Natura venne anche il capriccio   10
di creare, fra tanti, un animale
ch'io 'l guardo e rido, e di paura aggriccio.

Non ride ei già, ma con voce nasale
scilingua e ghigna s'altri gli contende;
di nessun dice bene, e d'ognun male.

Anzi, male per ben sempre ti rende:
ladro ti chiama di ciò ch'ei t'invola,
e per propria la tua merce rivende.

Trangugiasi volumi d'ogni scuola,
e un pasticcio latino-italo-greco   20
rivomita indigesto dalla gola.

Erra intorno cogli occhi, eppure è cieco;
da lunge annusa e corre al putridume;
grida dì e notte, e sempre come l'eco.

Striscia per andar dietro all'altrui lume;
se gli è presso, abbarbagliasi e nol vede:
striscia perché non ha gambe né piume.

Fu battezzato un dì, ma non ha fede;
né avrà salute mai, ché a mostri tali
l'eterna vita il Cielo non concede.   30

To Leopoldo Cicognara*

Let all, who want to, print their rhyming prose,   1
While you and your Lucia kindly study
This, which is destined for no ears but yours.

I think no one had ever set his hand
To comedy where laughter and repulsion
Were both aroused at monstrous humankind.

It seems that nature generally cuts off
Witty banter from downright detestation:
Judas gets hate; Narcissus gets a laugh.

Yet nature did indulge a whimsy here   10
In her creation of, among the beasts,
One forcing me to laugh, and shrink with fear.

Not that he laughs; but in a nasal tone
He snarls and stutters if he's ever challenged,
Speaking nothing but ill of everyone.

For good he renders evil in return;
He says you steal what he himself has stolen,
Then sells your goods as though they were his own.

He gulps heterogeneous volumes down
And then, in Greek-Italian-Latin, vomits   20
The undigested gobbets up again.

His eyes go rolling round, though he is blind;
He snuffles and he runs towards corruption;
He barks and barks, but only echoes sound.

He crawls behind another's guiding light;
Then, once he's near, he's dazzled, not enlightened;
He crawls since he has neither wings nor feet.

He was baptized, but he has no belief,
Nor will be saved; for to such monstrous beings
Heaven will never give eternal life.   30

21

E questo ha due peccati originali,
oltre quel d'Eva: dentro non ha cuore,
e di fuor non ha i fregi genitali.

D'impotente libidine d'amore
arrabbia quindi; e la venerea face
e l'apollinea desiando, muore.

Non sonno trova mai quando si giace,
ma l'altrui gioia delirando insidia,
e per turbarla a noi perde sua pace.

Quando l'Orgoglio si sposò l'Accidia,   40
fu concetto sotterra, e per nudrice,
che l'allattò di fiele, ebbe l'Invidia.

Poi grandicel succhiò certa radice
detta grammaticale, e fu creato
mastino all'eliconïa pendice.

Di catena brevissima allacciato,
a chi a poggiar gli passa da vicino
abbaia e ringhia tremante arrabbiato.

E a chi manca la lena a quel cammino
fa poi moine, e il chiama con la coda,   50
e chiede per limosina un quattrino.

Per fame ti vitupera e ti loda;
per fame ardisce e teme e liscia e morde;
fame gl'insegna a far bella ogni froda.

Ma ben più d'oro che di pane ha ingorde
le fauci: e spesso apparve alla mia vista
con monete d'umano sangue lorde.

Questo animal si chiama il Giornalista.

He has two sins which are original,
Besides the one from Eve: no heart inside,
And nothing outside that is genital.

In his libidinous impotence he flies
Into his rages and, desiring Venus
And that great art Apollo teaches, dies.

When he gets into bed he's so distressed
By others' joy he never falls asleep;
Disturbing *ours* he loses all *his* rest.

It was when Pride was wed to Accidie   40
He was conceived in secret, and his nurse,
Who suckled him with gall, was Jealousy.

Growing in size, he sucked grammatical
Roots, or ones thought such, and he then became
A watchdog on the Heliconian Hill.

And tethered as he is by a short chain,
He barks and howls and twitches in his anger
At anyone who passes on the climb.

If anyone gets breathless on that journey,
He makes a fuss of him and wags his tail,   50
And begs him for the handout of a penny.

For hunger he will praise, vituperate;
For hunger dare and fear, or stroke and snap;
And hunger makes him varnish all deceit.

His jaws are gaping more for gold than bread:
When he comes into view, then it is most
Often with lucre fouled with human blood.

This animal is called the *Journalist*.

Dal Paradise Lost *di Milton*

Dell'uom la prima inobbedienza e il frutto
dell'arbore vietata, onde l'assaggio
diede noi tutti a morte e all'infinite
miserie, lunge dal perduto Edenne,
finché l'uomo divino alle bëate
perdute sedi redentor ne assunse,
canta, o Musa celeste!…

*A Fragment Translated from Milton**

Of man's first disobedience, and the fruit
Of that forbidden tree, whose mortal taste
Brought death into the world, and all our woe,
With loss of Eden, till one greater man
Restore us, and regain the blissful seat,
Sing heavenly Muse…

A Luigia Pallavicini caduta da cavallo

I balsami beati   1
per te le Grazie apprestino,
per te i lini odorati
che a Citerea porgeano
quando profano spino
le punse il piè divino

quel dì che insana empiea
il sacro Ida di gemiti,
e col crine tergea
e bagnava di lagrime   10
il sanguinoso petto
al ciprio giovinetto.

Or te piangon gli amori,
te fra le dive liguri
regina e diva! E fiori
votivi all'ara portano
d'onde il grand'arco suona
del figlio di Latona.

E te chiama la danza
ove l'aure portavano   20
insolita fragranza
allor che a' nodi indocile
la chioma al roseo braccio
ti fu gentile impaccio.

Tal nel lavacro immersa,
che fiori dall'inachio
clivo cadendo versa,
Palla i dall'elmo liberi
crin su la man che gronda
contien fuori dall'onda.   30

To Luigia Pallavicini, Thrown from Her Horse*

May healing balms be brought   1
To you by the Three Graces,
Cool linen fragrance-fraught,
As with the Cytherean
That day when thorns profane
Defiled her foot divine,

That day she wildly groaned
On holy heights of Ida,
And with her tresses cleaned
In floods of lachrymation   10
That breast bedewed with blood
Of Cyprus' golden lad.*

The Loves lament and keen
Among Liguria's godheads
For you, goddess and queen!
With blossoms on that altar
Whereon the bow is seen
Of great Latona's son.*

Still you the dances summon,
Whence gentle gales were breathing   20
With fragrance more than human,
While your rebellious tresses
Were twining to no harm
Around each rosy arm.

Just so, bathed in the fount
Precipitating blossoms
From the Inachian mount,
Her loosened tresses Pallas
Contrives to hold above,
While her hand streams, the wave.   30

27

Armonïosi accenti
dal tuo labbro volavano,
e dagli occhi ridenti
traluceano di Venere
i disdegni e le paci,
la speme, il pianto e i baci.

Deh! perché hai le gentili
forme e l'ingegno docile
vòlto a studii virili?
Perché non dell'Aonie   40
seguivi, incauta, l'arte,
ma i ludi aspri di Marte?

Invan presaghi i venti
il polveroso agghiacciano
petto e le reni ardenti
dell'inquïeto alipede,
ed irritante il morso
accresce impeto al corso.

Ardon gli sguardi, fuma
la bocca, agita l'ardua   50
testa, vola la spuma,
ed i manti volubili
lorda, e l'incerto freno,
ed il candido seno;

e il sudor piove, e i crini
sul collo irti svolazzano,
suonan gli antri marini
allo incalzato scalpito
della zampa, che caccia
polve e sassi in sua traccia.   60

Già dal lito si slancia
sordo ai clamori e al fremito,
già già fino alla pancia

Accents of harmony
Out of your lips were fluttered;
From your eyes smilingly,
As from the orbs of Venus,
Shone high disdain and peace,
Hope, grieving and a kiss.

Alas! Why did you turn
Soft limbs, quick understanding
To pastimes meant for men?
And why not follow rather –   40
Too rash! – Aonian arts,
Than the rough games of Mars?

In vain did boding winds
Strive hard to cool the dusty
Breast and the ardent limbs
Of the rash beast, wing-footed,
Nor did the bit restrain,
But urged it on again.

Its eyeballs flash, its jaws
Steam, with the head uplifted;   50
Foam streams back as it flies
To soil her fluent garments,
Her breast once snowy-white,
Her hand that would clutch tight;

Sweat gleams; the horse's mane
Along its neck is bristling;
The ocean caves complain
At the insistent trampling
Of hooves which fling around
Stones on their dusty road.   60

It strikes out from the land,
Deaf to the shouts and terror,
The waters rise around,

29

nuota... e ingorde si gonfiano
non più memori l'acque
che una dea da lor nacque.

Se non che il re dell'onde,
dolente ancor d'Ippolito,
surse per le profonde
vie dal tirreno talamo,   70
e respinse il furente
col cenno onnipotente.

Quei dal flutto arretrosse
ricalcitrando e – orribile! –
sovra l'anche rizzosse;
scuote l'arcion, te misera
su la petrosa riva
strascinando mal viva.

Pèra chi osò primiero
discortese commettere   80
a infedele corsiero
l'agil fianco femineo,
e aprì con rio consiglio
nuovo a beltà periglio!

Ché or non vedrei le rose
del tuo volto sì languide,
non le luci amorose
spiar ne' guardi medici
speranza lusinghiera
della beltà primiera.   90

Di Cinzia il cocchio aurato
le cerve un dì traeano,
ma al ferino ululato
per terrore insanirono,
e dalla rupe etnea
precipitàr la dea.

It swims... the greedy ocean
Forgets that from its womb
A goddess was once born.*

The sovereign of the sea,
Hippolytus bewildered,*
Rose from profundity
Of his Tyrrhenian nuptials,   70
And drove it back again
With his almighty sign.

So driven back, the steed –
Oh spectacle of horror! –
Rose on its haunches, reared,
And shook you from the saddle,
And dragged you out of hand
Along the rocky strand.

Now may he have my curse,
That boor who first committed   80
To an unfaithful horse
A lady's gentle body,
Thereby only the more
Endangering the fair!

Else I'd not see the rose
Forsake your pallid visage,
Nor see your loving eyes
Seek in the doctors' glances
For some delusive chance
Of beauty you had once.   90

Cynthia* was in her coach,
Which hinds one day were drawing,
When at a bestial screech
Those hinds, o'ercome with terror,
From Etna's rocky crown
Hurtled the Goddess down.

Gioìan d'invido riso
le abitatrici olimpie,
perché l'eterno viso,
silenzïoso e pallido,   100
cinto apparia d'un velo
ai conviti del cielo;

ma ben piansero il giorno
che dalle danze efesie
lieta facea ritorno
fra le devote vergini,
e al ciel salia più bella
di Febo la sorella.

Olympians, envious
Of her, giggled in pleasure
At that immortal face,
Now silent grown and pallid,   100
Seen but through veily shrouds
At banquets in the clouds:

But how they rued the day
When from the Ephesian dances
She went up to the sky
With her devoted virgins,
Phoebus Apollo's sister,
More beautiful than ever!

Alla amica risanata

Qual dagli antri marini   1
l'astro più caro a Venere
co' rugiadosi crini
fra le fuggenti tenebre
appare, e il suo vïaggio
orna col lume dell'eterno raggio,

sorgon così tue dive
membra dall'egro talamo,
e in te beltà rivive,
l'aurea beltate ond'ebbero   10
ristoro unico a' mali
le nate a vaneggiar menti mortali.

Fiorir sul caro viso
veggo la rosa, tornano
i grandi occhi al sorriso
insidïando, e vegliano
per te in novelli pianti
trepide madri, e sospettose amanti.

Le Ore che dianzi meste
ministre eran de' farmachi,   20
oggi l'indica veste
e i monili cui gemmano
effigïati dei –
inclito studio di scalpelli achei –

e i candidi coturni
e gli amuleti recano
onde a' cori notturni
te, dea, mirando obbliano
i garzoni le danze,
te principio d'affanni e di speranze.   30

*To His Friend when She Was Restored to Health**

As from the ocean caves 1
That star most dear to Venus,*
Whose locks salt water laves,
Among the fleeting shadows
Rises, and on its way
Shines with the light of the eternal ray –

So you raise your divine
Limbs from their bed of sickness,
And beauty lives again,
Beauty which gave their only 10
Refreshment to the ill
Minds of mortals condemned to wander still.

On your dear countenance
I see fresh roses blooming;
Your large eyes once more glance
And captivate – and grieving
I see the anxious mothers,
Watching you always like suspicious lovers.

Careful the Hours* would bless
The sick with medication; 20
But now your Seric dress,
And cameos ornamented
With gods in effigy –
Those masterworks of Grecian artistry –

And cothurns gleaming bright,
And jewels the Hours are bringing –
All mean that every night
Young men forgo the dancing
To gaze at you, Goddess,
The fount of sorrow and of hopefulness. 30

O quando l'arpa adorni
e co' novelli numeri
e co' molli contorni
delle forme che facile
bisso seconda, e intanto
fra il basso sospirar vola il tuo canto

più periglioso; o quando
balli disegni, e l'agile
corpo all'aure fidando,
ignoti vezzi sfuggono   40
dai manti, e dal negletto
velo scomposto sul sommosso petto.

All'agitarti, lente
cascan le trecce, nitide
per ambrosia recente,
mal fide all'aureo pettine
e alla rosea ghirlanda
che or con l'alma salute april ti manda.

Così ancelle d'Amore
a te d'intorno volano   50
invidïate l'Ore;
meste le Grazie mirino
chi la beltà fugace
ti membra, e il giorno dell'eterna pace.

Mortale guidatrice
d'oceanine vergini,
la parrasia pendice
tenea la casta Artemide,
e fea – terror di cervi –
lungi fischiar d'arco cidonio i nervi.   60

Lei predicò la fama
olimpia prole; pavido
diva il mondo la chiama,

When you adorn the harp,
And with unwonted numbers,
And with your flowing shape
Flimsy lawn emphasizes,
With many sighs among,
All half-suppressed, you send out flights of song

More dangerous than beauty;
Oh when you dance, soft breezes
Encompassing your body,
Uncanny charms are wafted   40
From blown robes and distressed
Veils which but half conceal your heaving breast.

And as you move, your hair
Cascades in curls, still gleaming
With fresh ambrosia,
Escaping from the golden
Comb and the rosy crown –
April's award now you're restored again.

The everlasting Hours
Fly always round about you,   50
Love's grateful servitors.
The Graces are disheartened
To think how beauty flees
And how there is a day of lasting peace.

At first the mortal guide
Of nymphs that swim the ocean,
And on the mountainside
Parrhasian, chaste Artémis
Filled all the beasts with awe
To hear her Cretan bow hiss from afar.   60

Poets made her a child
Born on Olympus, goddess
To the whole awestruck world,

e le sacrò l'elisio
soglio ed il certo telo,
e i monti e il carro della luna in cielo.

Are così a Bellona,
un tempo invitta amazzone,
die' il vocale Elicona;
ella il cimiero e l'egida   70
or contro l'Anglia avara
e le cavalle ed il furor prepara.

E quella a cui di sacro
mirto te veggo cingere
devota il simolacro,
che presiede marmoreo
agli arcani tuoi lari
ove a me sol sacerdotessa appari,

regina fu: Citera
e Cipro – ove perpetua   80
odora primavera –
regnò beata, e l'isole
che col selvoso dorso
rompono agli euri e al grande Ionio il corso.

Ebbi in quel mar la culla:
ivi erra ignudo spirito
di Faon la fanciulla,
e se il notturno zeffiro
blando sui flutti spira,
suonano i liti un lamentar di lira;   90

ond'io, pien del nativo
aer sacro, su l'itala
grave cetra derivo
per te le corde eolie,
e avrai divina i voti
fra gl'inni miei delle insubri nipoti.

Queen of Elysian meadows,
Huntress who always hit,
And driver of the lunar chariot.*

So vocal Helicon
Raised altars to Bellona,*
All-conquering Amazon;
Now she with plume and aegis   70
'Gainst Albion and its greed
Prepares war's terrors and the trampling steed.*

And she, whose sacred head
I see that you with myrtle
Wreathe in your holy dread,
She the presiding marble*
In your most secret space,
And you the only priestess in that place,

Was the queen governing
Both Cyprus and Cythera   80
And everlasting spring,
And over all the islands
Which break with shaggy spine
The Eurus and the broad Ionian.*

In that sea I was born* –
Strays there a naked spirit,*
Phaon's sad girl, lovelorn,
And when at night the zephyr
Over its ripples blows,
A long-lamenting lyre sounds from its shores: 90

So, from my native air
For you I carry over
To the grave Italian lyre
These strings Aeolian:
You shall, from hymns of mine,
Be worshipped by the Lombards as divine.*

Le Grazie

Inno primo
Venere

Cantando, o Grazie, degli eterei pregi   1
di che il cielo v'adorna, e della gioia
che vereconde voi date alla terra –
belle vergini! – a voi chieggo l'arcana
armonïosa melodia pittrice
della vostra beltà, sì che all'Italia
afflitta di regali ire straniere
voli improvviso a rallegrarla il carme.
Nella convalle fra gli aerei poggi
di Bellosguardo, ov'io cinta d'un fonte   10
limpido fra le quete ombre di mille
giovinetti cipressi alle tre Dive
l'ara innalzo, e un fatidico laureto
in cui men verde serpeggia la vite
la protegge di tempio, al vago rito
vieni, o Canova, e agl'inni. Al cor men fece
dono la bella dea che in riva d'Arno
sacrasti alle tranquille arti custode;
ed ella d'immortal lume e d'ambrosia
la santa immago sua tutta precinse.   20
Forse (o ch'io spero!), artefice di numi,
nuovo meco darai spirto alle Grazie
ch'or di tua man sorgon dal marmo. Anch'io
pingo e spiro a' fantasmi anima eterna:
sdegno il verso che suona e che non crea;
perché Febo mi disse: "Io Fidia primo
ed Apelle guidai con la mia lira."
    Eran l'Olimpo e il Fulminante e il Fato,
e del tridente enosigèo tremava
la genitrice Terra; Amor dagli astri   30
Pluto ferìa: né ancor v'eran le Grazie.
Una diva scorrea lungo il creato
a fecondarlo, e di Natura avea

The Graces*

The First Hymn
Venus

Singing, O Graces, the celestial honours   1
High heaven adorns you with, and the delight
You in all modesty lend to the earth,
Lovely virgins! I beg from you the secret
Of that melodious vivid harmony
Embodied in your beauty; so my artless
Song may rejoice afflicted Italy,
Racked by the wrath of royal foreigners.*
Into the vale amidst the airy hills
Of Bellosguardo* – where, girt by a crystal   10
Lake and the silent shadows of a thousand
Young cypresses, I dedicate my altar
To the three goddesses, and where prophetic
Laurels embraced by vines of lighter green
Protect it like a temple – come, Canova,*
To glorious rites and hymns! These I received
From lovely Venus whom on Arno's banks
You consecrated to the arts pacific,
Where circumambient her sacred image
Is light immortal with ambrosia.   20
It is my hope that you, sculptor of gods,
Will give, with me, fresh spirit to the Graces
You call forth from the marble. For I too
Paint visions and breathe into them a soul:
I scorn verse that resounds without creating;
Phoebus has said to me: "I led the way
For Phidias and Apelles* with my lyre."
   Olympus and the Thunderer* and Fate
Were ruling; the Earthshaker's* trident shook
Our mother Earth; and Love from the high stars   30
Struck Pluto* down: there were as yet no Graces.
A goddess coursed throughout created things
To make them fruitful, and she had the name

41

l'austero nome: fra' celesti or gode
di cento troni, e con più nomi ed are
le dan rito i mortali; e più le giova
l'inno che bella Citerea la invoca.

Perché clemente a noi che mirò afflitti
travagliarci e adirati, un dì la santa
diva, all'uscir de' flutti ove s'immerse   40
a ravvivar le gregge di Nerèo,
apparì con le Grazie, e le raccolse
l'onda ionia primiera, onda che amica
del lito ameno e dell'ospite musco
da Citera ogni dì vien desìosa
a' materni miei colli: ivi fanciullo
la deità di Venere adorai.
Salve, Zacinto! All'antenoree prode,
de' santi lari idei ultimo albergo
e de' miei padri, darò i carmi e l'ossa,   50
e a te il pensier: ché pïamente a queste
dee non favella chi la patria obblia.
Sacra città è Zacinto. Eran suoi templi,
era ne' colli suoi l'ombra de' boschi
sacri al tripudio di Diana e al coro,
pria che Nettuno al reo Laomedonte
munisse Ilio di torri inclite in guerra.
Bella è Zacinto. A lei versan tesori
l'angliche navi; a lei dall'alto manda
i più vitali rai l'eterno sole;   60
candide nubi a lei Giove concede,
e selve ampie d'ulivi, e liberali
i colli di Lieo: rosea salute
prometton l'aure, da' spontanei fiori
alimentate, e da' perpetui cedri.

Splendea tutto quel mar quando sostenne
su la conchiglia assise e vezzeggiate
dalla diva le Grazie: e a sommo il flutto,
quante alla prima prima aura di Zefiro
le frotte delle vaghe api prorompono,   70
e più e più succedenti invide ronzano

Austere of Nature: now she has a hundred
Celestial thrones; with many names and altars
Mortals perform her rites; she takes most pleasure
In hymns invoking her as Cytherea.*
  In clemency to us whom she observed
In travails and in wrath, one day the sacred
Goddess, out of the waves where she had been   40
Arousing Nereus and his water-nymphs,
Rose up, with her the Graces, welcomed first
By the Ionian wave, that wave which, loving
The pleasing shore and the congenial flora,
Comes from Cythera daily in desire
To my maternal hills: there as a child
I worshipped the divinity of Venus.
Zante, all hail! To Antenorean coasts,
Ultimate refuge of the gods of Ida
And of my fathers, I give song and bones,   50
But you my thoughts: he cannot speak devoutly
With goddesses who slights his motherland.
Sacred is Zante. Her temples and her hills
And bosky shades were sacred to Diana
With her tripudium and choral nymphs,
Ere Neptune for the false Laomedon*
Built Ilium her towers renowned in war.
Lovely is Zante. Ships from Albion
Pour treasure into her; and from high heaven
Perpetual sunlight sheds its vital rays;   60
Jove has bestowed white shining clouds on her,
Broad olive groves and hillsides set apart
For Bacchus:* and a glow of rosy health
Is pledged by gentle gales instinct with flowers
Self sown and with her everlasting cedars.
  That sea was all resplendent when it bore
The Graces on a seashell cosseted
By Venus: on the surface of the flood –
As many as, when Zephyr starts to breathe,
Abounding swarms of bees are breaking out,   70
And wave on wave succeeds, impatient, buzzing

a far lunghi di sé aerei grappoli,
van alïando su' nettarei calici
e del mèle futuro in cor s'allegrano,
tante a fior dell'immensa onda raggiante
ardian mostrarsi a mezzo il petto ignude
le amorose Nereidi oceanine;
e a drappelli agilissime seguendo
la Gioia alata, degli dèi foriera,
gittavan perle, dell'ingenue Grazie   80
il bacio le Nereidi sospirando.
   Poi come l'orme della diva e il riso
delle vergini sue fêr di Citera
sacro il lito, un'ignota vïoletta
spuntò a' piè de' cipressi, e d'improvviso
molte purpuree rose amabilmente
si conversero in candide. Fu quindi
religïone di libar col latte
cinto di bianche rose, e cantar gl'inni
sotto a' cipressi, e d'offerire all'ara   90
le perle, e il primo fior nunzio d'aprile.
   L'una tosto alla dea col radïante
pettine asterge mollemente e intreccia
le chiome dell'azzurra onda stillanti.
L'altra ancella a le pure aure concede,
a rifiorire i prati a primavera,
l'ambrosio umore ond'è irrorato il petto
della figlia di Giove; vereconda
la lor sorella ricompone il peplo
su le membra divine, e le contende   100
di que' mortali attoniti al desio.
   Non prieghi d'inni o danze d'imenei,
ma de' veltri perpetuo l'ululato
tutta l'isola udia, e un suon di dardi
e gli uomini sul vinto orso rissosi,
e de' piagati cacciatori il grido.
Cerere invan donato avea l'aratro
a que' feroci: invan d'oltre l'Eufrate
chiamò un dì Bassareo, giovine dio,

To form aërial clusters far away
And hover o'er nectareous calyxes,
Rejoicing in their hearts at future honey –
So many, shining on the sea immense,
Nereides, made bold by love, discovered,
Or rather half-revealed, their naked breasts;
And following rapidly in sprightly bands
The wingèd Joy, harbinger of the Gods,
Shook pearl drops from themselves and sighed in longing   80
For kisses from the unpretentious Graces.
   When footprints of the Goddess and her laughing
Virgins had sanctified the Cytherean
Shore, then a little violet unknown
Sprang at the foot of cypresses; and sudden
A throng of purple roses pleasingly
Transfigured into white. It was thenceforth
Religion to libate with milk, engirdled
With whitest roses, and to sing the hymns
Under the cypresses, and strew the altar   90
With pearls and that first flower which heralds April.
   One of the Graces with her shining comb
Rinses gently and braids the Goddess' locks
Still oozing from the drench of azure waves.
The second Grace releases to the wind,
To fecundate the meadows in the Spring,
The ambrosial humour that bedews the breast
Of Jove's great offspring; while in modesty
Their sister rearranges the blown peplos
About the limbs divine, in strong contention   100
With the concupiscence of startled mortals.
   No prayers, no hymns, nor any nuptial dancing,
But hounds in never-ending ululation
Sounded throughout the isle, with hissing missiles,
With men at odds above a slaughtered bear,
With mingled cries from huntsmen who were wounded.
It was in vain Ceres* bestowed the plough
On these wild men: in vain beyond Euphrates
She called one day for Bacchus, the young god,

a ingentilir di pampini le rupi.   110
Il pio strumento irrugginia su' brevi
solchi, sdegnato; e divorata, innanzi
che i grappoli recenti imporporasse
a' rai d'autunno, era la vite: e solo
quando apparian le Grazie i cacciatori
e le vergini squallide e i fanciulli
l'arco e 'l terror deponeano, ammirando.

To civilize the rocks with planted vines.   110
The instrument, god-given, lay and rusted
On the truncated furrow; and the vine,
Before its latest clusters could empurple
In autumn sunlight, was devoured: and only
As the three Graces came in sight, did hunters
And unkempt maids and savage youths discard
Their terror and their weaponry, dumbfounded.

Sepulchres*

For Ippolito Pindemonte

*Deorum manium
iura sancta sunto.*
XII Tab.*

All'ombra de' cipressi e dentro l'urne   1
confortate di pianto è forse il sonno
della morte men duro? Ove più il sole
per me alla terra non fecondi questa
bella d'erbe famiglia e d'animali,
e quando vaghe di lusinghe innanzi
a me non danzeran l'ore future,
né da te, dolce amico, udrò più il verso
e la mesta armonia che lo governa,
né più nel cor mi parlerà lo spirto   10
delle vergini Muse e dell'amore –
unico spirto a mia vita raminga –
qual fia ristoro a' dì perduti un sasso
che distingua le mie dalle infinite
ossa che in terra e in mar semina morte?
Vero è ben, Pindemonte! Anche la Speme,
ultima dea, fugge i sepolcri, e involve
tutte cose l'obblio nella sua notte;
e una forza operosa le affatica
di moto in moto; e l'uomo e le sue tombe   20
e l'estreme sembianze e le reliquie
della terra e del ciel traveste il tempo.
    Ma perché pria del tempo a sé il mortale
invidierà l'illusïon che spento
pur lo sofferma al limitar di Dite?
Non vive ei forse anche sotterra, quando
gli sarà muta l'armonia del giorno,
se può destarla con soavi cure
nella mente de' suoi? Celeste è questa
corrispondenza d'amorosi sensi,   30
celeste dote è negli umani; e spesso
per lei si vive con l'amico estinto
e l'estinto con noi, se pia la terra
che lo raccolse infante e lo nutriva,
nel suo grembo materno ultimo asilo
porgendo, sacre le reliquie renda

Shaded by cypresses, and kept in urns,   1
Consoled by weeping, is the sleep of death
Really not quite so rigid? When the sun
For me at length no longer fills the earth
With such a family of plants and beasts,
And when the hours to come no longer dance
Bright and illusory before my eyes,
And when, dear friend, I hear your verse no longer
With that sad music which decides its rhythm,
And when the spirit in my heart no longer   10
Speaks of the virgin Muses and of love
(That spirit all that guides my wandering ways),
What solace for days lost would be a stone
Made to distinguish mine from other, countless
Bones which death scatters over land and sea?
For truly, Pindemonte, even Hope,
Last of the gods to go, deserts the tomb;
Oblivion draws all things into its night;
A force that never tires wears all things out,
Never at rest; and man and tombs of men,   20
The final shape of things, and the remains
Of land and sea are all transformed by time.
   But why – before time does – must man begrudge
Himself the illusion which, when he is dead,
Yet stops him at the doorway into Dis?*
Buried, does he not go on living, with
Day's harmony to him inaudible,
If he rouse this illusion with sweet care
In friendly memories? It is heaven-sent,
This correspondence of such deep affection,   30
A heavenly gift for human beings; and often
This means we go on living with our friend,
And he with us, if reverently the earth,
Which took him as a child and nourished him,
Offers a final refuge in her lap,
And keeps the sacredness of his remains

51

dall'insultar de' nembi e dal profano
piede del vulgo, e serbi un sasso il nome,
e di fiori odorata arbore amica
le ceneri di molli ombre consoli.   40
   Sol chi non lascia eredità d'affetti
poca gioia ha dell'urna; e se pur mira
dopo l'esequie, errar vede il suo spirto
fra 'l compianto de' templi acherontei,
o ricovrarsi sotto le grandi ale
del perdono d'Iddio: ma la sua polve
lascia alle ortiche di deserta gleba
ove né donna innamorata preghi,
né passeggier solingo oda il sospiro
che dal tumulo a noi manda Natura.   50
   Pur nuova legge impone oggi i sepolcri
fuor de' guardi pietosi, e il nome a' morti
contende. E senza tomba giace il tuo
sacerdote, o Talia, che a te cantando
nel suo povero tetto educò un lauro
con lungo amore, e t'appendea corone;
e tu gli ornavi del tuo riso i canti
che il lombardo pungean Sardanapàlo,
cui solo è dolce il muggito de' buoi
che dagli antri abdüani e dal Ticino   60
lo fan d'ozi beato e di vivande.
O bella Musa, ove sei tu? Non sento
spirar l'ambrosia, indizio del tuo nume,
fra queste piante ov'io siedo e sospiro
il mio tetto materno. E tu venivi
e sorridevi a lui sotto quel tiglio
ch'or con dimesse frondi va fremendo
perché non copre, o dea, l'urna del vecchio
cui già di calma era cortese e d'ombre.
Forse tu fra plebei tumuli guardi   70
vagolando ove dorma il sacro capo
del tuo Parini? A lui non ombre pose
tra le sue mura la città, lasciva
d'evirati cantori allettatrice,

From outrage of the storm-clouds and profane
Feet trampling, and a stone preserves his name,
And fragrantly in bloom a friendly tree
Comforts his ashes in its gentle shade.   40
   Only who leaves no legacy of love
Has little joy in urns; and should he look
Beyond the funeral rites, he sees his spirit
Straying lamenting in the infernal regions
Or sheltering underneath the enormous wings
Of God's forgiveness: but he leaves his dust
To nettles spreading on untended turf,
Where neither loving woman offers prayers,
Nor solitary traveller hears the sigh
Which Nature sends to us out of the tomb.   50
   And yet today's new law sets tombs apart
From reverent glances, and denies the dead
Their glorious name. So now, Thalia, your priest*
Is lying untombed who, singing in your praise
Under his poor roof, cultivated laurel
With constant love, and hung up crowns to you;
Your laugh adorned those songs of his which hit
The Sardanapalus* of Lombardy,
Whose only pleasure lies in lowing herds
From Adda's hollows and the broad Ticino   60
Blessing his idleness with food and drink.
Where are you, Muse? I do not catch the scent
Ambrosia breathes, the token of your presence,
Among these shades where I sit down to sigh
My mother's house. And yet you used to come
And smile at him beneath that very lime
Whose drooping foliage shakes and shudders since
It does not shroud the urn of that old man
To whom it always lent such peace and shade.
Perhaps you stray among the meanest graves,   70
Searching to find where sleeps the sacred head
Of your Parini? Not a tree to shade him
Inside that city's walls, that city* lewd
Enough to harbour enervated singers!

non pietra, non parola – e forse l'ossa
col mozzo capo gl'insanguìna il ladro
che lasciò sul patibolo i delitti.
Senti raspar fra le macerie e i bronchi
la derelitta cagna ramingando
su le fosse e famelica ululando;   80
e uscir del teschio, ove fuggia la luna,
l'ùpupa, e svolazzar su per le croci
sparse per la funerëa campagna,
e l'immonda accusar col luttüoso
singulto i rai di che son pie le stelle
alle obblïate sepolture. Indarno
sul tuo poeta, o dea, preghi rugiade
dalla squallida notte. Ahi! su gli estinti
non sorge fiore ove non sia d'umane
lodi onorato e d'amoroso pianto.   90
   Dal dì che nozze e tribunali ed are
dier alle umane belve esser pietose
di se stesse e d'altrui, toglieano i vivi
all'etere maligno ed alle fere
i miserandi avanzi che Natura
con veci eterne a sensi altri destina.
Testimonianza a' fasti eran le tombe,
ed are a' figli; e uscian quindi i responsi
de' domestici lari, e fu temuto
su la polve degli avi il giuramento: 100
religïon che con diversi riti
le virtù patrie e la pietà congiunta
tradussero per lungo ordine d'anni.
Non sempre i sassi sepolcrali a' templi
fean pavimento; né agl'incensi avvolto
de' cadaveri il lezzo i supplicanti
contaminò; né le città fur meste
d'effigïati scheletri: le madri
balzan ne' sonni esterrefatte, e tendono
nude le braccia su l'amato capo   110
del lor caro lattante onde nol desti
il gemer lungo di persona morta

No stone, no word! His bones may well be bloodied
By contact with the severed head of one
Who left his crimes but only on the scaffold.
You hear her scraping over thorns and rubble,
That sad abandoned bitch that roams around
Among the grave-pits, howling out of hunger;   80
You hear the hoopoe flutter from the skull
In which she shunned the moon, and flit through crosses
Scattered about the sombre countryside;
You hear that unclean bird reproach with mournful
Sobbing those rays the pitying starlight sheds
Upon forgotten graves. In vain, O Goddess,
You pray for dew to fall upon your poet
Out of the dreary night. Above the dead
No flower arises if it be not honoured
With human praises and with love's lament.   90
    When that day came when marriage, laws and altars
Gave to the human animal respect
Both for himself and others, then the living
From bitter weather and wild beasts abstracted
Those pitiful remains which Nature destines
To everlasting change and further ends.
Then tombs were witnesses to deeds of glory,
Altars for those who follow; from them came
The household gods' responses; oaths were awesome,
Oaths sworn upon the dust of ancestors: 100
This was the cult which, though the rites might vary,
The love of fatherland and family
Transmitted through the long succeeding years.
Not always have sepulchral stones been used
To pave our temples; nor involved in smoke
Of incense has the stench of corpses blighted
Those praying; nor have towns been always sad
With pictured skeletons (I see the mothers
Bound from their beds in terror, and extend
Their naked arms above the precious brows   110
Of their dear babies lest they be disturbed
By the protracted groaning of the dead

chiedente la venal prece agli eredi
dal santüario. Ma cipressi e cedri,
di puri effluvi i zefiri impregnando,
perenne verde protendean su l'urne
per memoria perenne, e prezïosi
vasi accogliean le lagrime votive.
Rapian gli amici una favilla al sole
a illuminar la sotterranea notte,   120
perché gli occhi dell'uom cercan morendo
il sole, e tutti l'ultimo sospiro
mandano i petti alla fuggente luce.
Le fontane, versando acque lustrali,
amaranti educavano e vïole
su la funebre zolla; e chi sedea
a libar latte e a raccontar sue pene
ai cari estinti una fragranza intorno
sentia qual d'aura de' beati Elisi.
Pietosa insania che fa cari gli orti   130
de' suburbani avelli alle britanne
vergini, dove le conduce amore
della perduta madre, ove clementi
pregaro i Geni del ritorno al prode
che tronca fe' la trïonfata nave
del maggior pino, e si scavò la bara.
Ma ove dorme il furor d'inclite gesta
e sien ministri al vivere civile
l'opulenza e il tremore, inutil pompa
e inaugurate immagini dell'Orco   140
sorgon cippi e marmorei monumenti.
Già il dotto e il ricco ed il patrizio vulgo,
decoro e mente al bello italo regno,
nelle adulate reggie ha sepoltura
già vivo, e i stemmi unica laude. A noi
morte apparecchi riposato albergo
ove una volta la fortuna cessi
dalle vendette, e l'amistà raccolga
non di tesori eredità, ma caldi
sensi e di liberal carme l'esempio.   150

Who beg their heirs to buy a prayer for them
Out of the sanctuary); but cypresses
And cedars, loading zephyrs with their scent,
Stretched everlasting green above the urns
In everlasting memory, and precious
Vases were there to take the votive tears.
Friends used to snatch a sparkle from the sun
To illuminate the subterranean dark,   120
Because the eyes of dying men search out
The sun, and every breast exhales at last
One final sigh towards the light that flies.
Springs, always pouring out their lustral waters,
Fostered the amaranth and violet
On the funereal turf; and he who sat there,
To offer bowls of milk and tell his grief
To the departed, sensed a fragrance round,
As though a breeze that breathed Elysium.
A fond illusion! Which endears suburban   130
Gardens of tombs to girls who grieve in Britain;
They, guided to those gardens by the love
Of their dead mothers, linger to beg mercy
From spirits of homecoming for the hero*
Who had the captured ship truncated by
Its tallest mast, and hollowed thence his coffin.
But where the rage for fame lies sound asleep,
Where opulence and dread are ministers
To civic living, then mere useless pomp,
Or worse, ill-omened images of Orcus,*   140
Are monumental pillars made from marble.
The learned already, and the rich and noble –
The mind and ornament of Italy –
Are tombed alive in sycophantic courts,
Armorial bearings all their praise. For us
May death prepare a place where we may rest,
Where fortune in the course of time must cease
From persecution; and may friendship gather
No heritage of hoarded wealth, but warmth
Of sentiment and independent song.   150

57

A egregie cose il forte animo accendono
l'urne de' forti, o Pindemonte; e bella
e santa fanno al peregrin la terra
che le ricetta. Io quando il monumento
vidi ove posa il corpo di quel grande
che temprando lo scettro a' regnatori
gli allòr ne sfronda, ed alle genti svela
di che lagrime grondi e di che sangue,
e l'arca di colui che nuovo Olimpo
alzò in Roma a' Celesti, e di chi vide   160
sotto l'etereo padiglion rotarsi
più mondi, e il sole irradïarli immoto –
onde all'Anglo che tanta ala vi stese
sgombrò primo le vie del firmamento –
"Te beata," gridai, "per le felici
aure pregne di vita, e pe' lavacri
che da' suoi gioghi a te versa Apennino!"
Lieta dell'aer tuo veste la luna
di luce limpidissima i tuoi colli
per vendemmia festanti, e le convalli   170
popolate di case e d'oliveti
mille di fiori al ciel mandano incensi:
e tu prima, Firenze, udivi il carme
che allegrò l'ira al Ghibellin fuggiasco,
e tu i cari parenti e l'idïoma
désti a quel dolce di Calliope labbro
che Amore in Grecia nudo e nudo in Roma
d'un velo candidissimo adornando
rendea nel grembo a Venere Celeste;
ma più beata che in un tempio accolte   180
serbi l'itale glorie, uniche forse
da che le mal vietate Alpi e l'alterna
onnipotenza delle umane sorti
armi e sostanze t'invadeano ed are
e patria e, tranne la memoria, tutto.
Ché ove speme di gloria agli animosi
intelletti rifulga ed all'Italia,
quindi trarrem gli auspici. E a questi marmi

The urns of strong men stimulate strong minds
To deeds of great distinction; and these urns
Make sacred for the traveller that earth
Which holds them. When I saw the monument
Where lies the body of that famous man*
Who, teaching rulers how to wield the sceptre,
Strips laurel from it, and reveals to all
What tears it drips with and what drops of blood;
And saw the tomb of him who raised in Rome
A new Olympus;* and the tomb of him   160
Who saw new worlds spin through the vaulted ether
Enlightened by the sun that shines unmoved* –
And, for the Englishman* to spread his wings,
First cleared the pathways of the firmament –
Then I cried: "Bless you Florence for your gentle
Breezes so full of life, and for your waters
Running from ridges of the Apennines!"
Happy in such an atmosphere the moon
Clothes with her clearest light your clustered hills
Where grapes are gathering; and from your valleys,   170
Crowded with houses and with olive-groves,
The incense of a thousand flowers goes up.
You were the first to hear the song that eased
The anger of the exiled Ghibelline;*
And you gave parents and an idiom
To him through whom Calliope was vocal,
Who clothing Love in veils of purest white –
Naked in Greece, naked in ancient Rome –
Restored Love to the lap of Heaven's Venus.*
Blessèd because one temple* still preserves   180
Italy's glories, and her only glories
Now that the ill-defended Alps and all
The variability of human fate
Have spoilt her of her arms and wealth and altars
And nationhood, and left but memory.
When hope of glory comes to shine at last
On ardent intellects of Italy
We shall draw portents hence. And to these marbles

59

venne spesso Vittorio ad ispirarsi.
Irato a' patrii numi, errava muto   190
ove Arno è più deserto, i campi e il cielo
desïoso mirando; e poi che nullo
vivente aspetto gli molcea la cura,
qui posava l'austero, e avea sul volto
il pallor della morte e la speranza.
Con questi grandi abita eterno: e l'ossa
fremono amor di patria. Ah sì! da quella
religïosa pace un nume parla:
e nutria contro a' Persi in Maratona,
ove Atene sacrò tombe a' suoi prodi,   200
la virtù greca e l'ira. Il navigante
che veleggiò quel mar sotto l'Eubea
vedea per l'ampia oscurità scintille
balenar d'elmi e di cozzanti brandi,
fumar le pire igneo vapor, corrusche
d'armi ferree vedea larve guerriere
cercar la pugna; e all'orror de' notturni
silenzi si spandea lungo ne' campi
di falangi un tumulto e un suon di tube
e un incalzar di cavalli accorrenti,   210
scalpitanti su gli elmi a' moribondi,
e pianto ed inni, e delle Parche il canto.

    Felice te che il regno ampio de' venti,
Ippolito, a' tuoi verdi anni correvi!
E se il piloto ti drizzò l'antenna
oltre l'isole egèe, d'antichi fatti
certo udisti suonar dell'Ellesponto
i liti, e la marea mugghiar portando
alle prode retèe l'armi d'Achille
sovra l'ossa d'Ajace: a' generosi   220
giusta di glorie dispensiera è morte;
né senno astuto né favor di regi
all'Itaco le spoglie ardue serbava,
ché alla poppa raminga le ritolse
l'onda incitata dagl'inferni dei.

    E me, che i tempi e il desio d'onore

Vittorio* often came for inspiration.
Angry with his own land, he wandered silent   190
Where Arno is deserted, looking longing
At fields and sky; and when he found no sight
Or living thing to mitigate his grief,
That stern man halted here, upon his face
Death-pallor manifest and also hope.
With these great men for ever, he inspires
Love of his native land. Oh, out of that
Religious peace there is a spirit speaking:
It nursed against the Medes at Marathon,
Where Athens dedicated tombs to heroes,   200
Greek valour and Greek ire. The mariner
Sailing that sea which lies beneath Euboea
Observed beyond the spacious dark the lightning
Of flashing helmets and of clashing swords,
The pyres of blazing smoke, and saw the shapes
Of spectral warriors in burnished arms
Seek out the battle; heard grim silence shattered
By uproar of the phalanxes extending
Into the plains by night, a sound of trumpets,
A constant press of horses rushing up   210
To trample on the helmets of the dying,
Lament, and triumph, and the singing Fates.
   How fortunate, Ippolito, when young,
To roam the spacious sea, the realm of winds!
And if the helmsman ever steered your ship
Beyond the Aegean Isles, you must have heard
The shores that line the Hellespont resound
With ancient deeds, heard the tide roar which washed
Achilles' arms up on the Trojan beach
Above the bones of Ajax. Death is just   220
In giving glory to the noble-hearted:
Not all his wiliness, no prince's favours,
Could keep Ulysses master of those spoils
Won with such effort; waves the gods below
Aroused removed them from his wandering ship.
   I, whom the times and appetite for honour

61

fan per diversa gente ir fuggitivo,
me ad evocar gli eroi chiamin le Muse,
del mortale pensiero animatrici.
Siedon custodi de' sepolcri, e quando   230
il tempo con sue fredde ale vi spazza
fin le rovine, le Pimplèe fan lieti
di lor canto i deserti, e l'armonia
vince di mille secoli il silenzio.
Ed oggi nella Troade inseminata
eterno splende a' peregrini un loco,
eterno per la ninfa a cui fu sposo
Giove, ed a Giove die' Dàrdano figlio,
onde fur Troia e Assàraco e i cinquanta
talami e il regno della giulia gente.   240
Però che quando Elettra udì la Parca
che lei dalle vitali aure del giorno
chiamava a' cori dell'Eliso, a Giove
mandò il voto supremo: "E se," diceva,
"a te fur care le mie chiome e il viso
e le dolci vigilie, e non mi assente
premio miglior la volontà de' fati,
la morta amica almen guarda dal cielo,
onde d'Elettra tua resti la fama."
Così orando moriva. E ne gemea   250
l'Olimpio, e l'immortal capo accennando
piovea dai crini ambrosia su la ninfa,
e fe' sacro quel corpo e la sua tomba.
Ivi posò Erittonio, e dorme il giusto
cenere d'Ilo; ivi l'iliache donne
sciogliean le chiome, indarno ahi! deprecando
da' lor mariti l'imminente fato;
ivi Cassandra, allor che il nume in petto
le fea parlar di Troia il dì mortale,
venne; e all'ombre cantò carme amoroso,   260
e guidava i nepoti, e l'amoroso
apprendeva lamento a' giovinetti.
E dicea sospirando: "Oh se mai d'Argo,
ove al Tidìde e di Laerte al figlio

Impel through diverse peoples as an exile,
I pray the Muses help me call up heroes,
The Muses who enliven mortal thought.
They sit as guardians of tombs; and when   230
Time with his chilly wings has swept away
The ruins even, then the Muses make
The deserts glad with song, and overcome
The silence of a thousand centuries.
Even today one place in barren Troas
Is still a wonder to the traveller,
Eternized by the nymph who lay with Jove
And gave to Jove a son – that Dardanus
From whom came Tros, Assaracus, the fifty
Sons of great Priam, and the Julian line.   240
For when the nymph Electra heard the Fates
Calling her from the vital air of day
To the Elysian choirs, she breathed to Jove
A final prayer. "And if," she said, "you ever
Cherished my tresses, and my face, those nights
We lay awake in love, and if harsh fate
Withholds from me the best reward of all,
At least protect your dead friend out of heaven,
That fame of your Electra may survive."
And with that prayer she died. The Olympian   250
Was moved and, bowing his immortal head,
He rained ambrosia down upon the nymph
And made her body sacred and her tomb.
There Erichthonius* lay, and there the ashes
Of Ilus* rested; there the Trojan women
Would loose their hair, in vain alas, to pray for
Their husbands to avoid the impending fate;
Cassandra when the deity within her
Forced her to prophesy Troy's mortal day,
Came there, and sang the shades a loving song,   260
And brought them their descendants, and instructed
The young men in the threnody of love.
She said with sighs: "If ever out of Argos,
Where you will act as herdsmen for the horses

63

pascerete i cavalli, a voi permetta
ritorno il cielo, invan la patria vostra
cercherete! Le mura, opra di Febo,
sotto le lor reliquie fumeranno.
Ma i penati di Troia avranno stanza
in queste tombe; ché de' numi è dono   270
servar nelle miserie altero nome.
E voi, palme e cipressi che le nuore
piantan di Priamo, e crescerete ahi presto
di vedovili lagrime innaffiati,
proteggete i miei padri: e chi la scure
asterrà pio dalle devote frondi
men si dorrà di consanguinei lutti,
e santamente toccherà l'altare.
Proteggete i miei padri. Un dì vedrete
mendico un cieco errar sotto le vostre   280
antichissime ombre, e brancolando
penetrar negli avelli, e abbracciar l'urne,
e interrogarle. Gemeranno gli antri
secreti, e tutta narrerà la tomba
Ilio raso due volte e due risorto
splendidamente su le mute vie
per far più bello l'ultimo trofeo
ai fatati Pelìdi. Il sacro vate,
placando quelle afflitte alme col canto,
i prenci argivi eternerà per quante   290
abbraccia terre il gran padre Oceàno.
E tu onore di pianti, Ettore, avrai
ove fia santo e lagrimato il sangue
per la patria versato, e finché il sole
risplenderà su le sciagure umane."

Of hard Ulysses, pitying Heavens permit
That you return here, you will look in vain
To find your native land! The very walls,
The work of Phoebus, will be smoking rubble.
But gods, the gods of Troy, will have a home
Within these tombs; it is a gift gods have,   270
To keep their proud name in the worst of plights.
And you, you palms and cypresses – whom Priam's
Daughters-in-law have planted, who will grow,
Too soon alas, watered by widows' tears –
Protect my ancestors! He who abstains
His axe from your devoted leaves will have
The less to mourn for from his flesh and blood,
And he will touch the altar with pure hands.
Protect my ancestors. The day will come
When you will see an old blind beggar* wander   280
Under your ancient shades, and feel his way
Into the burial place, and clasp the urns
And question them. Then all the hidden caves
Will murmur, and the mausoleum will tell
Of Ilium twice razed and twice arisen
In splendour high above the silent roadways
So that the final triumph might be greater
Won by the fateful Greeks. The sacred poet,
Soothing those troubled spirits with his song,
Will make the Argive kings immortal over   290
All lands embraced by the great father, Ocean.
And you, Hector, will have your meed of mourning
Wherever men hold holy and lament
The blood shed for the homeland, while the sun
Continues shining over human grief."

Note on the Text

Unless otherwise stated in the notes, all the translations have been made from Ugo Foscolo, *Poesie e Sepolcri*, edited by Donatella Martinelli (Milan: Arnoldo Mondadori, 1987).

Notes

p. 5, *I*: Publ. 1802.

p. 7, *II*: Publ. 1802.

p. 7, *Myrtle*: Symbol of love.

p. 7, *laurel*: Symbol of poetry.

p. 9, *III*: Publ. 1803.

p. 11, *IV*: Written 1801.

p. 11, *that city*: Florence.

p. 11, *papal... Ghibelline*: A clash in 1300 on the Ponte Santa Trinità between the White Guelfs and the Black Guelfs. Although both were supporters of the Pope, the White Guelfs were not wholly against the Emperor, which may be the reason why Foscolo uses the term Ghibelline (a pro-empire, anti-papacy faction).

p. 11, *home... bard*: Vittorio Alfieri (1749–1803), poet, playwright and patriot, lived on the Lungarno Corsini at the north end of the Ponte Santa Trinità.

p. 13, *V*: Written 1803.

p. 13, *brother*: Giovanni Foscolo died in 1801, it is said by stabbing himself in his mother's presence.

p. 15, *VI*: Written 1802–3.

p. 15, *he*: Homer.

p. 15, *famed verse*: The Odyssey.

p. 19, *Against Lamberti*: Translated from the Gori edition of Foscolo. In 1803 Lamberti was commissioned by the Italian Republic, with a substantial advance, to produce an edition of Homer, to be printed by Bodoni: nothing was completed until 1809, and then only the *Iliad*.

p. 21, *To Leopoldo Cicognara*: Translated from the UTET edition of Foscolo. Included in a letter of 1813 to Cicognara, who was a politician and soldier, the poem is directed against the priest and journalist Urbano Lampredi, who made a habit of attacking Foscolo.

p. 25, *A Fragment Translated from Milton*: From the Gori edition of of Foscolo. This fragment is included to give, in a brief space, some notion of Foscolo's powers as a translator. It is easy to point out where his rendering falls short: he fails to translate the word "mortal" in the second line and thus loses a powerful pun ("by man" and "lethal"); and "l'uomo divino" is a serious mistranslation, since Milton is careful to use the word "greater" which, while it does not stress his Arianism, does not contradict it either. Nevertheless, Foscolo's version is eloquent, and eloquent in a Miltonic way, especially in his reproduction of Milton's periodic sentence. The results of his reading of Milton are shown at their best in his *Sepulchres* and the elegant complexity of its syntax.

p. 27, *To Luigia... Horse*: Publ. 1800. The addressee was a young married woman whose beauty was irretrievably marred by her accident.

p. 27, *Cyprus' golden lad*: Adonis, loved by Venus and killed by a wild boar.

p. 27, *Latona's son*: Apollo, god of healing.

p. 31, *once born*: Venus was born out of the sea near the island of Cythera (see line 4).

p. 31, *Hippolytus bewildered*: That is, *whom* Hippolytus bewildered. Neptune was still grieving for Hippolytus, unjustly accused of rape, to whom he had sent a sea monster which frightened the horses drawing his chariot and caused his death.

p. 31, *Cynthia*: Diana, goddess of hunting.

p. 35, *To His Friend... Health*: Publ. 1803.

p. 35, *Venus*: Lucifer, the morning star.

p. 35, *Hours*: Attendants on Venus.

p. 39, *driver... chariot*: Artemis, goddess of hunting, is often identified with the moon. She is here represented as a mortal who was deified by the poets.

p. 39, *Bellona*: A Roman war goddess.

p. 39, *Prepares... trampling steed*: This alludes to the French preparations for renewed war with Britain after the Treaty of Amiens (signed in March 1802).

p. 39, *marble*: A statue of Venus.

p. 39, *Eurus... Ionian*: The east or south-east wind and the Ionian Sea.

p. 39, *born*: On the island of Zante.

p. 39, *spirit*: The poet Sappho (*fl.* 7th century BC).

p. 39, *worshipped… divine*: The woman to whom the poem is addressed was from Milan.

p. 41, *Graces*: Written 1813. Translated from UTET edition of Foscolo. This is the beginning only of a long poem which remained fragmentary.

p. 41, *Racked… foreigners*: The Napoleonic Wars, and particularly the invasion of Russia in 1812: there were Italians in Napoleon's invasion force.

p. 41, *Bellosguardo*: Hill to the south-west of Florence, where Foscolo lived during the first half of 1813.

p. 41, *Canova*: The sculptor Antonio Canova (1757–1822) who had made a statue of Venus for Florence.

p. 41, *Phidias… Apelles*: Representing respectively sculpture and painting.

p. 41, *Thunderer*: Jupiter.

p. 41, *Earthshaker's trident*: Neptune's sign of authority.

p. 41, *Pluto*: God of the Underworld.

p. 43, *Cytherea*: Venus, born near the island of Cythera.

p. 43, *false Laomedon*: Mythical King of Troy who failed to pay the sea god for building the walls of the city.

p. 43, *Bacchus*: God of wine, used here to signify grapes.

p. 45, *Ceres*: Goddess of earth's fruits and especially corn.

p. 49, *Sepulchres*: Written in 1806, after some discussion of burial customs with the poet Ippolito Pindemonte (1753–1828), and as a response to the current application to Italy of Napoleon's Edict of Saint Cloud (1804), which imposed burial outside inhabited areas, and plainness and uniformity of graves, on all classes of people.

p. 49, *XII Tab.*: *The rights of the sacred shades must be inviolable. (The Twelve Tables)*. The Twelve Tables were a code of Roman law published 451–450 BC.

p. 51, *Dis*: The underworld.

p. 53, *your priest*: The poet Giuseppe Parini (1729–99).

p. 53, *Sardanapalus*: An effeminate King of Assyria, denoting here the idle Lombard aristocracy.

p. 53, *that city*: Milan.

p. 57, *hero*: Horatio Nelson (1758–1805).

p. 57, *Orcus*: Another name for the underworld.

p. 59, *famous man*: Niccolò Machiavelli (1469–1527).

p. 59, *him who… new Olympus*: Michelangelo (1475–1564), the architect of St Peter's in Rome.

p. 59, *him… shines unmoved*: Galileo Galilei (1564–1642).

p. 59, *Englishman*: Isaac Newton (1642–1727).

p. 59, *Ghibelline*: Dante Alighieri (1265–1321). Although he was in fact a White Guelf, the fact that he was not staunchly against the Emperor and was critical of several popes may have led Foscolo to label him a Ghibelline.

p. 59, *To him… Heaven's Venus*: Francis Petrarch (1304–74).

p. 59, *one temple*: The Basilica of Santa Croce in Florence.

p. 61, *Vittorio*: See fourth note for p. 11.

p. 63, *Erichthonius*: A descendant of Electra.

p. 63, *Ilus*: Another descendant of Electra.

p. 65, *blind beggar*: Homer.

Extra Material

on

Ugo Foscolo's

Sepulchres

Ugo Foscolo's Life

Niccolò Foscolo (who in his teens changed his forename *Birth and Early Years*
to Ugo) was born in 1778 on the Ionian Island of Zante
(Zakynthos) to a Greek mother and a Venetian father. In 1784
the family moved to Split in Dalmatia, where his father worked
as a doctor and where Ugo had his early education. With the
death of the father in 1788 the family moved back to Zante.
Four years later, Ugo followed his mother to Venice.

These early moves set the pattern of his life, for Foscolo was
an exile several times over. Before he finally left his adopted
country at the age of thirty-seven, he had moved from city to
city and state to state in Italy. Linguistically his early years were
of great benefit to him: he grew up with Greek and Venetian,
and was educated in Classical Greek and Latin. It was later in
life that he acquired his knowledge of Tuscan – the language in
which he wrote – and English. His early experiences may have
encouraged a natural restlessness: they certainly had other
great and lasting effects on his cast of mind. His unswerving
love of liberty was influenced by his studies in ancient Greek,
and Zante, his birthplace, remained in his memory as a source
of pride, since it gave him a close connection with Greek an-
tiquity, and became for him an image of classical beauty and
harmony. At the same time, and with no apparent sense of
incongruity, he was a devoted Italian patriot, a patriot of that
country which then did not exist as a political entity and was
united and became self-governing only after his death.

Given those firm political and patriotic convictions, Foscolo *Political Convictions*
may seem at times to have been inconsistent in his actions.
This inconsistency, or rather ambivalence, is really an attribute
of the times themselves, and it illustrates how hard it was for
many people then, especially in continental Europe, to steer

73

a straight course. In some ways Foscolo is exemplary. This can be seen in his attitude to the French Revolution, which broke out when he was a little boy, and later in his attitude to Napoleon. It is customary when speaking of English writers of that period to note whether they welcomed the Revolution or not, and then whether they continued to rejoice in it after the Terror, and especially after it threw up a ruler whose tyranny was even more thorough than that of the Bourbons, because so much more intelligent and efficient. Wordsworth and Coleridge welcomed the Revolution, and then turned against it. Hazlitt remained its supporter, opposed Britain's wars with France, and never lost his admiration of Napoleon. It will be noticed that none of those writers' lives was inextricably mixed up with the cruel events in France and later in Europe as a whole, and their political views have a touch of the theoretical about them. Foscolo is more comparable with Heinrich Heine, another poet who saw the effects of the Revolution at close quarters. When as a child Heine watched the triumphal entry of French troops into his home town of Düsseldorf, he was told by his mother that this meant civic rights for them as Jews, and when he was a man he still hero-worshipped Napoleon. Foscolo saw Napoleon as the one person who might free Italy from the Austrians and facilitate its unification. It is understandable then that after Napoleon's invasion of Italy in 1796 Foscolo should enlist in his army and fight for him. During the following years he continued to nourish the vain hope that Napoleon would be a liberator and not a tyrant, and continued to support him even under arms. This was far from being a wholehearted admiration, however: on many occasions he criticized Napoleon severely and publicly.

Move to the Euganean Hills In 1796 Foscolo found it politically dangerous to remain in Venice and took refuge outside Padua in the Euganean Hills, where he began work on what was to become *Ultime lettere di Jacopo Ortis* (*Last Letters of Jacopo Ortis*), one of his most important works. It was many years before it was finished: as always, politics kept breaking in.

By 1797 there was a large stretch of Italian territory, the Cisalpine Republic with its capital in Milan, which looked as though it might become the nucleus of a united country; but Foscolo's hopes and those of many others were frustrated later in the same year with the Treaty of Campoformio, by which Napoleon ceded Venice to Austria, using his conquered Italian territories merely as a bargaining chip. Then early in 1799 Piedmont was annexed by France.

Foscolo moved first to Milan and then to Bologna and resumed his work on the *Ortis*; but this was again interrupted by a call to arms in defence of the Republic against Austria, and he fought in several battles of this campaign. He also republished an earlier ode to Napoleon, accompanying it with an open letter urging him not to be a tyrant.

After Napoleon's victory over the Austrians at the Battle of Marengo in 1800, Foscolo returned to Milan as a captain in the army of the French. The next few years were occupied with several love affairs, the writing of sonnets, and the publication of the definitive edition of *Last Letters of Jacopo Ortis*. Since this is an epistolary novel, and since it tells of a young man's unhappy love and ultimate suicide, it is hard to avoid comparison with Goethe's *The Sorrows of Young Werther*, but the comparison must not be stretched too far. Goethe's work achieved European fame, whereas Foscolo's, although famous in Italy, was more limited in its appeal. In a sense its very limitations are its strength: Ortis cannot marry the young woman whom he loves and who loves him because her father must marry her off to someone who can mend the family's fortunes, and also protect them from political persecution. This mixture of private and public concerns gives the book much of its power, which is increased by the sense that unhappiness is not unusual, but rather the fate of human beings throughout the ages.

Publication of Last Letters of Jacopo Ortis

Foscolo was in Northern France from 1804 to 1806 as an infantry captain in the Napoleonic force which was intended for the invasion of England, but which in the event did not sail. During this time Foscolo had an affair with a young Englishwoman which resulted in the birth of a daughter. He successfully translated Laurence Sterne's *Sentimental Journey* into Italian, and began a translation of the *Iliad* which did not progress beyond the third book.

Service in the Napoleonic Army

In 1806, back in Italy, he composed his blank-verse masterpiece, *De' sepolcri (Sepulchres)*. The appeal of this poem is timeless; but the circumstances of its composition show clearly Foscolo's audacity and independence in a difficult historical situation. Its immediate inspiration was an edict issued by Napoleon while he was at the height of his power, and Foscolo challenges the edict head on.

Sepulchres

75

Ajax and
The Graces

In 1811, after his tragedy *Ajace* (*Ajax*) had failed on the stage and was then banned for political reasons, Foscolo was encouraged to leave Milan for his own good, and he went to Bellosguardo, just outside Florence, where he lived from 1812 to 1813 and where most of *Le Grazie* (*The Graces*) was written: unfortunately this poem remained unfinished.

After Napoleon's resounding defeat in the Battle of the Nations at Leipzig in 1813 at the hands of the Austrians, Prussians and Russians, Foscolo rejoined the Napoleonic army to defend what was by now the Kingdom of Italy, whose existence still gave him hope of an independent and united country. However, by 1813 the Austrians were in Milan. Foscolo hesitated whether to accord them his allegiance, but decided not to, and in 1815 he left Italy for good, going first to Switzerland, and then to England where he settled.

Exile in England
and Death

In England he had a very different welcome from the one that would have been his if he had arrived in 1806: he was fêted as a celebrity, since his criticism of Napoleon was well known. However, this happy period did not last long. From his journalism and critical essays such as those on Dante, Petrarch and Boccaccio he made more than enough money to live on, but not enough to keep him in the lavish style of life he wished for, and so he was constantly in debt. He was joined in England by his daughter, and he wasted the money she had inherited from her grandmother on the building of a luxurious villa which subsequently had to be sold to meet his debts. He died in poverty in Turnham Green and was buried in Chiswick Cemetery. His grave can still be seen there, but his remains were removed in 1871, after the unification of Italy, and reburied in Santa Croce in Florence, among those of other famous Italians he had praised in *Sepulchres*. The survival of his fame as an Italian poet and patriot was confirmed in 1939, when the Italian government had a statue placed over his tomb in Santa Croce. It shows him as a wounded but defiant warrior.

Ugo Foscolo's Poetry

Foscolo's poetry is uneven in quality. His most ambitious poem, *The Graces*, consists of fragments only. Yet he did leave behind a substantial body of masterly work dealing with complex subjects in a refined and polished manner.

In his best poetry, the strong tendency to histrionic self-pity, most evident in the fictional, but only lightly disguised, character of Jacopo Ortis, is artistically controlled and balanced by self-knowledge and self-criticism. This balance is shown in the sonnets translated here, and especially in that which begins:

> No, I'll not land upon your sacred shore,
> Zante, ever again!…

The same thought is amplified at the end of this sonnet:

> …My doom
> Is exile and an unwept sepulchre.

In between, the classical references and allusions are not mere fashionable ornament but serve to universalize Foscolo's personal plight.

Such classical references are a recurrent feature of his poetry, working sometimes to make of the poem a rather precious and idealized object, and at their best widening the poem's scope beyond the personal and into history. There is still such a strong tendency in English criticism after Wordsworth to decry any diction that may be described as "artificial" that it is worthwhile recalling that Leopardi (in his *Zibaldone* 3418) praised Foscolo's language and style because it was "more precisely and more perfectly poetical and distinct from prose than that of any other of our poets." Poetry is an art, and what is artistic is always to some extent artificial: how artificial one likes it is a matter of taste.

The odes 'To Luigia Pallavicini, Thrown from Her Horse' and 'To His Friend when She Was Restored to Health' are so crowded with classical references that on first reading it may be difficult to work out precisely what the poet is on about. A natural response of the English reader might well be to ask:

> Must all be veiled, while he that reads, divines,
> Catching the sense at two removes?
> (George Herbert, 'Jordan')

Both poems are ultimately quite clear however, and if the reader decides that they are more in the nature of *objets d'art* than anything else – why not? They are reminiscent of Gray or Collins at their least direct and most artificial, and it has seemed best to translate them into that idiom. This is poetry on stilts, but it does have its attractions, as stilt-walking always does. There are moreover hints, especially in the second of these poems, of something with much greater depth. The mention there of "Albion in its greed" and of the preparations for "war's terrors" comes close to being a flaw in the poem, since the contemporary reference jars somewhat in these rather precious surroundings, but it does foreshadow that combination of contemporary and fictional classical worlds which is so successful later in 'Sepulchres'. There is also in this second poem a pregnant suggestion that it is poets who create the gods, and therefore the moral and other qualities the gods personify. Since Foscolo does not believe those qualities have any divine sanction, it may be said that he puts classical allusions into his poems to promote what he sees as illusions; but for him these are such illusions as are necessary for noble and civilized living, and they are remarkably persistent throughout history. Shades of Leopardi!

Foscolo's most typical and also his best characteristics are evident in 'Sepulchres'. Because of its allusiveness and rapid transitions and its involved, although always exact, syntax, it is again not easy on a first reading, or indeed even on several readings. All its idiosyncrasies are, however, in the end triumphantly justified. This is a very unusual poem in its theme and in its method. Since it concerns itself with tombs and graveyards, Thomas Gray may well spring to mind; but the tenor of the poem is quite different from that of the 'Elegy Written in a Country Churchyard'. It takes its first impulse not from an imagined rural scene at twilight, but from a harsh Napoleonic edict imposing burial outside inhabited areas and plainness and uniformity of graves; it moves then throughout history, both actual and mythical, contemporary (with Nelson and Parini) and past (with the Battle of Marathon), to what is not only an elaborate and forceful condemnation of that edict, but the revelation of a whole *Weltanschauung*. The theme can be stated simply: Foscolo sees no life after death except the physical transmutation of our remains into other existences; but tombs can perpetuate the memory of the dead, not merely for sentimental reasons – the "correspondence of such deep affection" – but for the noble dead to be kept in mind as an incitement to noble actions on the part of their descendants:

The urns of strong men stimulate strong minds
To deeds of great distinction; and these urns
Make sacred for the traveller that earth
Which holds them…

Foscolo would certainly have agreed with the pronouncement by Pericles, in his famous funeral oration over the Athenian dead in the Peloponnesian War, that "the whole earth is the tomb of famous men"; but he was insistent also on the need for some physical reminder to keep the memory fresh of who these dead were and what they did. The bald statement of the theme does not do justice to the wealth of illustration and evidence which Foscolo accumulates, or to the rhetorical skill his poem reveals. And as the very existence of this poem shows, the arts have their part to play in these acts of commemoration, since

…The muses make
The deserts glad with song, and overcome
The silence of a thousand centuries.

Select Bibliography

Editions of Foscolo:
Foscolo, Ugo, *Opere poetiche*, ed. Pietro Gori (Florence: Salani, 1886)
Foscolo, Ugo, *Poesie e prose d'arte*, ed. Enzo Bottasso, 3rd edn. (Turin: UTET, 1968)
Foscolo, Ugo, *Poesie e Sepolcri*, ed. Donatella Martinelli (Milan: Arnoldo Mondadori, 1987)
Foscolo, Ugo, *Last Letters of Jacopo Ortis*, tr. J.G. Nichols (London: Hesperus Press, 2002)

Additional Recommended Background Reading:
Cambon, Glauco, *Ugo Foscolo, Poet of Exile* (Princeton, NJ: Princeton University Press, 1980).
Vincent, Eric Reginald Pearce, *Ugo Foscolo: An Italian in Regency England* (Cambridge, Cambridge University Press, 1953)

Appendix

This poem (taken from the Gori edition of Foscolo) was written in 1820, while Foscolo was living in England. It was addressed to a young Englishwoman, Caroline Russell, which is presumably why he wrote it in English. Of the six classical figures called Callirhoe, Foscolo probably had in mind the one who rejected the love of Coresus, as a result of which the latter killed himself.

To Callirhoe

Her face was veil'd. Yet to my fancied sight
Love, sweetness, goodness in her person shin'd…
But oh!…
I wak'd…

John Milton

I twine, far distant from my Tuscan grove,   1
The lily chaste, the rose that breathes of love,
The myrtle leaf and Laura's hallow'd bay,
The deathless flow'rs that bloom o'er Sappho's clay;

For thee, Callirhoe! – Yet by Love and years
I learn how Fancy wakes from joy to tears;
How Memory pensive, 'reft of hope, attends
The Exile's path, and bids him fear new friends.

Long may the garland blend its varying hue
With thy bright tresses, and bud ever-new   10
With all Spring's odours; with Spring's light be dressed,
Inhale pure fragrance from thy virgin breast!

And when thou find'st that Youth and Beauty fly
As heavenly meteors from our dazzled eye,
Still may the garland shed perfume, and shine
While Laura's mind and Sappho's heart are thine.

ALMA CLASSICS

ALMA CLASSICS aims to publish mainstream and lesser-known European classics in an innovative and striking way, while employing the highest editorial and production standards. By way of a unique approach the range offers much more, both visually and textually, than readers have come to expect from contemporary classics publishing.

༄

1. James Hanley, *Boy*
2. D.H. Lawrence, *The First Women in Love*
3. Charlotte Brontë, *Jane Eyre*
4. Jane Austen, *Pride and Prejudice*
5. Emily Brontë, *Wuthering Heights*
6. Anton Chekhov, *Sakhalin Island*
7. Giuseppe Gioacchino Belli, *Sonnets*
8. Jack Kerouac, *Beat Generation*
9. Charles Dickens, *Great Expectations*
10. Jane Austen, *Emma*
11. Wilkie Collins, *The Moonstone*
12. D.H. Lawrence, *The Second Lady Chatterley's Lover*
13. Jonathan Swift, *The Benefit of Farting Explained*
14. Anonymous, *Dirty Limericks*
15. Henry Miller, *The World of Sex*
16. Jeremias Gotthelf, *The Black Spider*
17. Oscar Wilde, *The Picture Of Dorian Gray*
18. Erasmus, *Praise of Folly*
19. Henry Miller, *Quiet Days in Clichy*
20. Cecco Angiolieri, *Sonnets*
21. Fyodor Dostoevsky, *Humiliated and Insulted*
22. Jane Austen, *Sense and Sensibility*
23. Theodor Storm, *Immensee*
24. Ugo Foscolo, *Sepulchres*
25. Boileau, *Art of Poetry*
26. Georg Kaiser, *Plays Vol. 1*
27. Émile Zola, *Ladies' Delight*
28. D.H. Lawrence, *Selected Letters*

To order any of our titles and for up-to-date information about our current and forthcoming publications, please visit our website on:

www.almaclassics.com

29673233R00056

Printed in Great
Britain
by Amazon